D1237881

Hippocrene
CHILDREN'S
ILLUSTRATED
GERMAN
DICTIONARY

ENGLISH - GERMAN
GERMAN - ENGLISH

Compiled and translated by the Editors of Hippocrene Books

Interior illustrations by S. Grant (24, 81, 88); J. Gress (page 10, 21, 24, 37, 46, 54, 59, 65, 72, 75, 77);
K. Migliorelli (page 13, 14, 18, 19, 20, 21, 22, 25, 31, 32, 37, 39, 40, 46, 47, 66, 71, 75, 76, 82, 86, 87);
B. Swidzinska (page 9, 11, 12, 13, 14, 16, 23, 27, 28, 30, 32, 33, 35, 37, 38, 41, 42, 45, 46, 47, 48, 49, 50, 52,
53, 56, 57, 58, 59, 60, 61, 62, 63, 66, 68, 69, 70, 71, 72, 73, 75, 77, 78, 79, 83), N. Zhukov (page 8, 13, 14,
17, 18, 23, 27, 29, 33, 34, 39, 40, 41, 52, 64, 65, 71, 72, 73, 78, 84, 86, 88).

Design, prepress, and production: Graafiset International, Inc.

Copyright © 1999 by Hippocrene Books, Inc.

All rights reserved.

Cataloging-in-Publication Data available from the Library of Congress.

ISBN 0-7818-0722-0

Printed in Hong Kong.

For information, address:
Hippocrene Books, Inc.
171 Madison Avenue
New York, NY 10016

INTRODUCTION

With their absorbent minds, infinite curiosities and excellent memories, children have enormous capacities to master many languages. All they need is exposure and encouragement.

The easiest way to learn a foreign language is to simulate the same natural method by which a child learns English. The natural technique is built on the concept that language is representational of concrete objects and ideas. The use of pictures and words are the natural way for children to begin to acquire a new language.

The concept of this Illustrated Dictionary is to allow children to build vocabulary and initial competency naturally. Looking at the pictorial content of the Dictionary and saying and matching the words in connection to the drawings gives children the opportunity to discover the foreign language and thus, a new way to communicate.

The drawings in the Dictionary are designed to capture children's imaginations and make the learning process interesting and entertaining, as children return to a word and picture repeatedly until they begin to recognize it.

The beautiful images and clear presentation make this dictionary a wonderful tool for unlocking your child's multilingual potential.

Deborah Dumont, M.A., M.Ed.,
Child Psychologist and Educational Consultant

German Pronunciation

Letter(s)	Pronunciation system used
a	**ah** like the *a* in English 'art'
ä	**ay** like the *a* in English 'angry'
au	**ou** as in English 'house'
b	**b** as in English 'bent' **p** at the end of a word or syllable as in English 'pull'
ch˙	**ch** like the guttural *ch* in the Scottish pronunciation of 'loch'
ch	**kh** a hissing sound formed by pressing the tongue to the lower front teeth and letting air pass between tongue and palate
chs	**x** as in English 'wax'
d	**d** as in English 'day' **t** at the end of a word or syllable as in English 'went'
e	**e** a short dull sound like the *e* in English 'panel'
eh	**eh** a long dull sound similar to the *e* in English 'legend'
ei	**igh** or **eye** as in English 'high' or 'eye'
er	**are** as in English 'hare' but shorter
eu	**oy** as in English 'boy'
f	**f** as in English 'fire'
g	**g** as in English 'give' at the end of a word or syllable like in English 'leek'
h	**h** as in English 'hand'. This letter is also used to lengthen a vowel.
i	**i** as in English 'ring' when short **ee** as in English 'see' when long

Letter(s)	Pronunciation system used
j	**y** as in English 'yesterday'
k	**k** as in English 'key'
l	**l** as in English 'land'
m	**m** as in English 'man'
n	**n** as in English 'no'
o	**o** like the short *o* in English 'pot'
o	**oh** like the long *o* in English 'corner'
ö	**oe** an o-sound formed by pursing both lips
p	**p** as in English 'pet'
q	**q** as in English 'quarter'
r	**r** an r-sound formed by pressing the tongue to the soft palate
s	**z** like the *z* in English 'zebra'
s	**s** like the hissing *s* in English 'beside'
sch	**sh** as in English 'ship'
t	**t** as in English 'today'
u	**oo** as in English 'book'
ü	**ooh** an u-sound formed by pursing both lips
v	**f** as in English 'fly'
w	**v** as in English 'view'
z	**ts** like the z in English 'waltz'

airplane **(das) Flugzeug**
(dahs) flook-tsoyk

alligator **(der) Alligator**
(dare) ahl-li-gah-tohr

alphabet **(das) Alphabet**
(dahs) ahl-fah-beht

antelope **(die) Antilope**
(dee) ahn-ti-loh-pe

antlers **(das) Geweih**
(dahs) ge-vigh

apple   **(der) Apfel**
(dare) ahp-fel

aquarium   **(das) Aquarium**
(dahs) ahk-vah-ri-yum

arch   **(der) Torbogen**
(dare) tohr-boh-gen

arrow   **(der) Pfeil**
(dare) pfile

autumn   **(der) Herbst**
(dare) hairpst

baby **(das) Baby**
(dahs) beh-bee

backpack **(der) Rucksack**
(dare) rook-zak

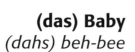

badger **(der) Dachs**
(dare) dahx

baker **(der) Bäcker**
(dare) bayk-kare

ball **(der) Ball**
(dare) bal

balloon **(der) Luftballon**
(dare) looft-bal-long

banana **(die) Banane**
(dee) bah-nah-ne

barley **(die) Gerste**
(dee) gare-ste

barrel **(das) Fass**
(dahs) fas

basket **(der) Korb**
(dare) kohrp

bat **(die) Fledermaus**
(dee) fleh-dare-mous

beach **(der) Strand**
(dare) shtrahnt

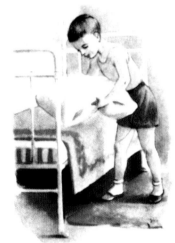

bear   **(der) Bär**
(dare) bayr

beaver   **(der) Biber**
(dare) bee-bare

bed   **(das) Bett**
(das) bet

bee   **(die) Biene**
(dee) bee-ne

beetle   **(der) Käfer**
(dare) kay-fare

bell   **(die) Glocke**
(dee) glok-ke

belt   **(der) Gürtel**
(dare) goohr-tel

bench   **(die) Bank**
(dee) bahnk

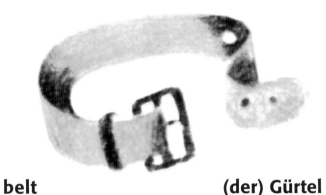

bicycle   **(das) Fahrrad**
(dahs) fahr-raht

binoculars   **(das) Fernglas**
(das) fern-glahs

bird   **(der) Vogel**
(dare) foh-gel

birdcage   **(der) Vogelkäfig**
(dare) foh-gel-kay-fik

black   **schwarz**
shvahrts

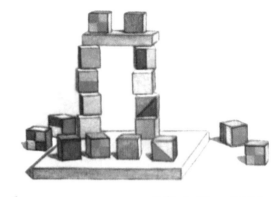

blocks   **(die) Bauklötze**
(dee) bou-kloet-se

blossom   **(die) Blüte**
(dee) blooh-te

blue   **blau**
blou

boat   **(das) Boot**
(dahs) boht

bone   **(der) Knochen**
(dare) kno-chen

book (das) Buch
(dahs) booch

boot (der) Stiefel
(dare) shtee-fel

bottle (die) Flasche
(dee) flah-she

bowl (die) Schüssel
(dee) shoohs-sel

boy (der) Junge
(dare) yoon-ge

bracelet (das) Armband
(dahs) ahrm-bahnt

branch **(der) Ast**
(dare) ahst

bread **(das) Brot**
(dahs) broht

breakfast **(das) Frühstück**
(dahs) frooh-shtoohk

bridge **(die) Brücke**
(dee) broohk-ke

broom **(der) Besen**
(dare) beh-zen

brother **(der) Bruder**
(dare) broo-dare

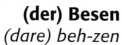

brown **braun**
broun

brush **(die) Bürste**
(dee) boohr-ste

bucket **(der) Eimer**
(dare) eye-mare

bulletin board **(das) schwarze Brett**
(dahs) shvahrt-se bret

bumblebee **(die) Hummel**
(dee) hoom-mel

butterfly **(der) Schmetterling**
(dare) shmet-tare-ling

cab   **(das) Taxi**
(dahs) tahk-see

cabbage   **(der) Kohl**
(dare) kohl

cactus   **(der) Kaktus**
(dare) kahk-toos

café   **(das) Café**
(dahs) kah-fey

cake   **(die) Torte**
(dee) tohr-te

camel   **(das) Kamel**
(dahs) kah-mayle

camera   **(die) Kamera**
(dee) kah-me-rah

candle   **(die) Kerze**
(dee) kare-tse

candy   **(das) Bonbon**
(dahs) bon-bong

canoe   **(das) Kanu**
(dahs) kah-noo

cap   **(die) Mütze**
(dee) mooht-se

captain   **(der) Kapitän**
(dare) kah-pi-tayn

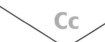

Cc

car   **(das) Auto**
(dahs) ou-toh

card   **(die) Spielkarte**
(dee) shpeel-kahr-te

carpet   **(der) Teppich**
(dare) tep-pikh

carrot   **(die) Karotte**
(dee) kah-rot-te

(to) carry   **tragen**
trah-gen

castle   **(das) Schloss**
(das) shlos

cat **(die) Katze**
(dee) kaht-se

cave **(die) Höhle**
(dee) hoe-le

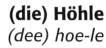

chair **(der) Stuhl**
(dare) shtool

cheese **(der) Käse**
(dare) kay-se

cherry **(die) Kirsche**
(dee) kir-she

chimney **(der) Schornstein**
(dare) shohrn-shtine

chocolate   **(die) Schokolade**
(dee) shoh-koh-lah-de

Christmas tree (der) Weihnachtsbaum
(dare) vigh-nachts-boum

circus   **(der) Zirkus**
(dare) tsir-koos

(to) climb   **klettern**
klet-tern

cloud   **(die) Wolke**
(dee) vol-ke

clown   **(der) Clown**
(dare) kloun

coach **(die) Kutsche**
(dee) koot-she

coat **(der) Mantel**
(dare) mahn-tel

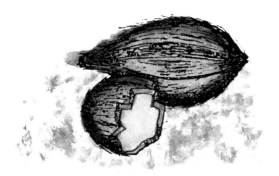

coconut **(die) Kokosnuss**
(dee) koh-kos-noos

comb **(der) Kamm**
(dare) kam

comforter **(die) Bettdecke**
(dee) bet-dek-ke

compass **(der) Kompass**
(dare) kom-pas

(to) cook kochen
ko-chen

cork **(der) Korken**
(dare) kohr-ken

corn **(der) Mais**
(dare) mice

cow **(die) Kuh**
(dee) koo

cracker **(der) Kräcker**
(dare) kray-kare

cradle **(die Wiege)**
(dee) vee-ge

(to) crawl   **krabbeln**
krab-beln

(to) cross   **überqueren**
ooh-bare-kveh-ren

crown   **(die) Krone**
(dee) kroh-ne

(to) cry   **weinen**
vigh-nen

cucumber   **(die) Gurke**
(dee) goor-ke

curtain   **(die) Gardine**
(dee) gahr-dee-ne

(to) dance   **tanzen**
tahn-tsen

dandelion   **(der) Löwenzahn**
(dare) loe-ven-tsahn

date   **(das) Datum**
(dahs) dah-toom

deer   **(das) Reh**
(dahs) reh

desert   **(die) Wüste**
(dee) vooh-ste

desk   **(der) Schreibtisch**
(dare) shripe-tish

dirty   **schmutzig**
shmoot-tsik

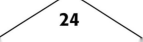

Dd

24

dog

(der) Hund
(dare) hoont

doghouse

(die) Hundehütte
(dee) hoon-de-hooht-te

doll

(die) Puppe
(dee) poop-pe

dollhouse

(das) Puppenhaus
(dahs) poop-pen-hous

dolphin

(der) Delphin
(dare) del-feen

donkey

(der) Esel
(dare) eh-sel

dragon

(der) Drache
(dare) drah-che

dragonfly (die) Libelle
(dee) lee-bel-le

(to) draw zeichnen
tseikh-nen

dress (das) Kleid
(dahs) klight

(to) drink trinken
trin-ken

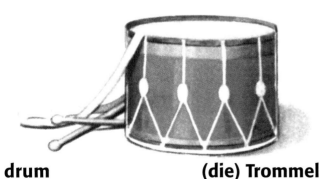

drum (die) Trommel
(dee) trom-mel

duck (die) Ente
(dee) en-te

eagle **(der) Adler**
(dare) ahd-lare

(to) eat **essen**
es-sen

egg **(das) Ei**
(dahs) eye

eggplant **(die) Aubergine**
(die) oh-bare-jee-ne

eight **acht**
acht

elbow **(der) Ellbogen**
(dare) el-boh-gen

elephant **(der) Elefant**
(dare) e-le-fahnt

empty   **leer**
lehr

engine   **(die) Lokomotive**
(dee) loh-koh-moh-tee-ve

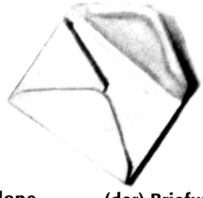

envelope   **(der) Briefumschlag**
(dare) breef-oom-shlahk

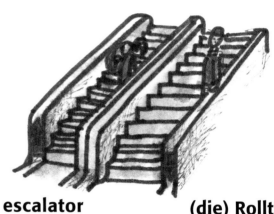

escalator   **(die) Rolltreppe**
(dee) rol-trep-pe

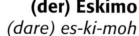

Eskimo   **(der) Eskimo**
(dare) es-ki-moh

(to) explore   **erforschen**
are-for-shen

eye   **(das) Auge**
(dahs) ou-ge

face   **(das) Gesicht**
(dahs) ge-zikht

fan   **(der) Ventilator**
(dare) ven-ti-lah-tohr

father   **(der) Vater**
(dare) fah-tare

fear   **(die) Angst**
(dee) ahnkst

feather   **(die) Feder**
(dee) feh-dare

(to) feed   **füttern**
fooht-tern

fence   **(der) Zaun**
(dare) tsoun

fern   **(der) Farn**
(dare) fahrn

field   **(das) Feld**
(dahs) felt

field mouse   **(die) Feldmaus**
(dee) felt-mous

finger   **(der) Finger**
(dare) fin-gare

fir tree   **(die) Tanne**
(dee) tan-ne

fire   **(das) Feuer**
(dahs) foyer

fish   **(der) Fisch**
(dare) fish

(to) fish   **angeln**
ahn-geln

fist   **(die) Faust**
(dee) foust

five   **fünf**
foohnf

flag   **(die) Flagge**
(dee) flag-ge

flashlight **(die) Taschenlampe**
(dee) tah-shen-lahm-pe

(to) float **treiben**
trigh-ben

flower **(die) Blume**
(dee) bloo-me

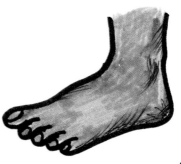

(to) fly **fliegen**
flee-gen

foot **(der) Fuß**
(dare) foos

fork **(die) Gabel**
(dee) gah-bel

fountain **(der) Brunnen**
(dare) broon-nen

four **vier**
feer

fox  **(der) Fuchs**
(dare) foox

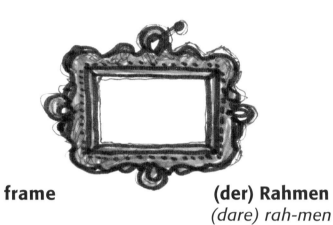

frame **(der) Rahmen**
(dare) rah-men

friend **(der) Freund**
(dare) froynt

frog **(der) Frosch**
(dare) frosh

fruit **(das) Obst**
(dahs) ohbst

furniture **(die) Möbel**
(dee) moe-bel

garden   **(der) Garten**
(dare) gahr-ten

gate   **(das) Tor**
(dahs) tohr

(to) gather   **sammeln**
sam-meln

geranium   **(die) Geranie**
(dee) geh-rah-ni-ye

giraffe   **(die) Giraffe**
(dee) gi-raf-fe

girl   **(das) Mädchen**
(dahs) mayd-khen

(to) give **geben**
geh-ben

glass **(das) Glas**
(dahs) glahs

glasses **(die) Brille**
(dee) bril-le

globe **(der) Globus**
(dare) gloh-boos

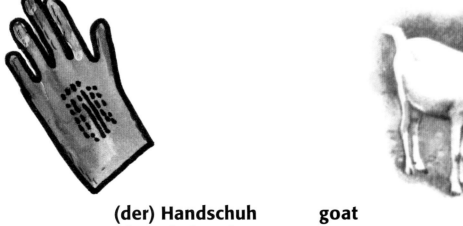

glove **(der) Handschuh**
(dare) hahnt-shoo

goat **(die) Ziege**
(dee) tsee-ge

goldfish   **(der) Goldfisch**
(dare) gold-fish

"Good Night"   **"Gute Nacht"**
goo-te nacht

"Good-bye"   **"Auf Wiedersehen"**
ouf vee-dare-seh-hen

goose   **(die) Gans**
(dee) gahns

grandfather   **(der) Großvater**
(dare) grohs-fah-tare

grandmother   **(die) Großmutter**
(dee) grohs-moot-tare

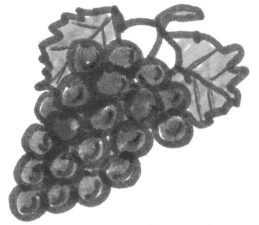

grapes   **(die) Weintrauben**
                    (dee) vine-trou-ben

grasshopper   **(der) Grashüpfer**
                         (dare) gras-hoohp-fare

green   **grün**
                   groohn

greenhouse   **(das) Gewächshaus**
                        (dahs) ge-vayx-hous

guitar   **(die) Gitarre**
                    (dee) gi-tar-re

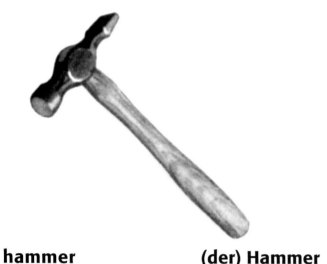

hammer   **(der) Hammer**
(dare) ham-mare

hammock   **(die) Hängematte**
(dee) hayn-ge-mat-te

hamster   **(der) Hamster**
(dare) hahm-stare

hand   **(die) Hand**
(dee) hahnt

handbag   **(die) Handtasche**
(dee) hahnt-tah-she

handkerchief   **(das) Taschentuch**
(dahs) tah-shen-tooch

harvest **(die) Ernte**
(dee) ern-te

hat **(der) Hut**
(dare) hoot

hay **(das) Heu**
(dahs) hoy

headdress **(der) Kopfschmuck**
(dare) kopf-shmook

heart **(das) Herz**
(dahs) hayrts

hedgehog **(der) Igel**
(dare) ee-gel

hen   **(die) Henne**
(dee) hen-ne

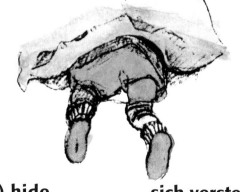

(to) hide   **sich verstecken**
sikh fare-shtek-ken

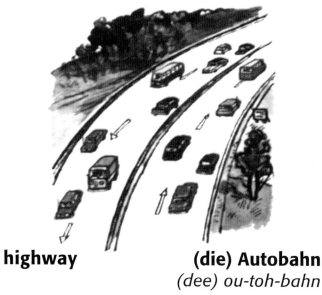

highway   **(die) Autobahn**
(dee) ou-toh-bahn

honey   **(der) Honig**
(dare) hoh-nik

horns   **(die) Hörner**
(dee) hoer-nare

horse   **(das) Pferd**
(dahs) pfehrd

horseshoe   **(das) Hufeisen**
(dahs) hoof-eye-sen

hourglass   **(die) Eieruhr**
(dee) eye-yare-oor

house   **(das) Haus**
(dahs) hous

(to) hug   **umarmen**
oom-ahr-men

hydrant   **(der) Hydrant**
(dare) hooh-drahnt

ice cream   **(das) Eis**
(das) eyes

ice cubes   **(die) Eiswürfel**
(dee) eyes-voohr-fel

ice-skating   **Eislaufen**
eyes-lou-fen

instrument   **(das) Instrument**
(dahs) in-stroo-ment

iris   **(die) Iris**
(dee) ee-ris

iron   **(das) Bügeleisen**
(dahs) booh-gel-eye-zen

island   **(die) Insel**
(dee) in-zel

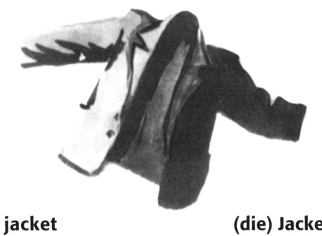

jacket   **(die) Jacke**
(dee) yak-ke

jam   **(die) Marmelade**
(dee) mahr-me-lah-de

jigsaw puzzle   **(das) Puzzlespiel**
(dahs) pu-zayl-shpeel

jockey   **(der) Jockey**
(dare) jok-key

juggler   **(der) Jongleur**
(dare) jon-gloer

(to) jump   **springen**
shprin-gen

kangaroo **(das) Kängeruh**
(dahs) kayn-ge-roo

key **(der) Schlüssel**
(dare) shloohs-sel

kitten **(das) Kätzchen**
(dahs) kayts-khen

knife **(das) Messer**
(dahs) mes-sare

knight **(der) Ritter**
(dare) rit-tare

(to) knit **stricken**
shtrik-ken

knot **(der) Knoten**
(dare) knoh-ten

koala bear **(der) Koalabär**
(dare) koh-ah-lah-bayr

ladder   **(die) Leiter**
(dee) ligh-tare

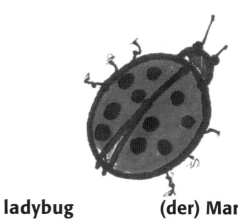

ladybug   **(der) Marienkäfer**
(dare) mah-ree-yen-kay-fare

lamb   **(das) Lamm**
(dahs) lam

lamp   **(die) Lampe**
(dee) lahm-pe

(to) lap   **auflecken**
ouf-lek-ken

laughter   **(das) Lachen**
(dahs) lah-chen

lavender   **(der) Lavendel**
(dare) lah-ven-del

lawn mower   **(der) Rasenmäher**
(dare) rah-zen-may-hare

leaf   **(das) Blatt**
(dahs) blat

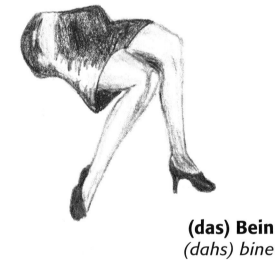

leg   **(das) Bein**
(dahs) bine

lemon   **(die) Zitrone**
(dee) tsi-troh-ne

lettuce   **(der) Salat**
(dare) zah-laht

lightbulb   **(die) Glühbirne**
(dee) glooh-bir-ne

lighthouse   **(der) Leuchtturm**
(dare) loykht-toorm

lilac   **(der) Flieder**
(dare) flee-dare

lion   **(der) Löwe**
(dare) loe-ve

(to) listen   **zuhören**
tsoo-hoe-ren

lobster   **(der) Hummer**
(dare) hoom-mare

lock   **(das) Türschloss**
(dahs) toohr-shlos

lovebird   **(der) Wellensittich**
(dare) vel-len-zit-tikh

luggage   **(das) Gepäck**
(dahs) ge-payk

lumberjack   **(der) Holzfäller**
(dare) holts-fayl-lare

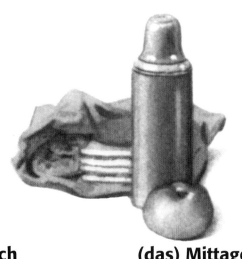 

lunch   **(das) Mittagessen**
(dahs) mit-tahk-es-sen

lynx   **(der) Luchs**
(dare) loox

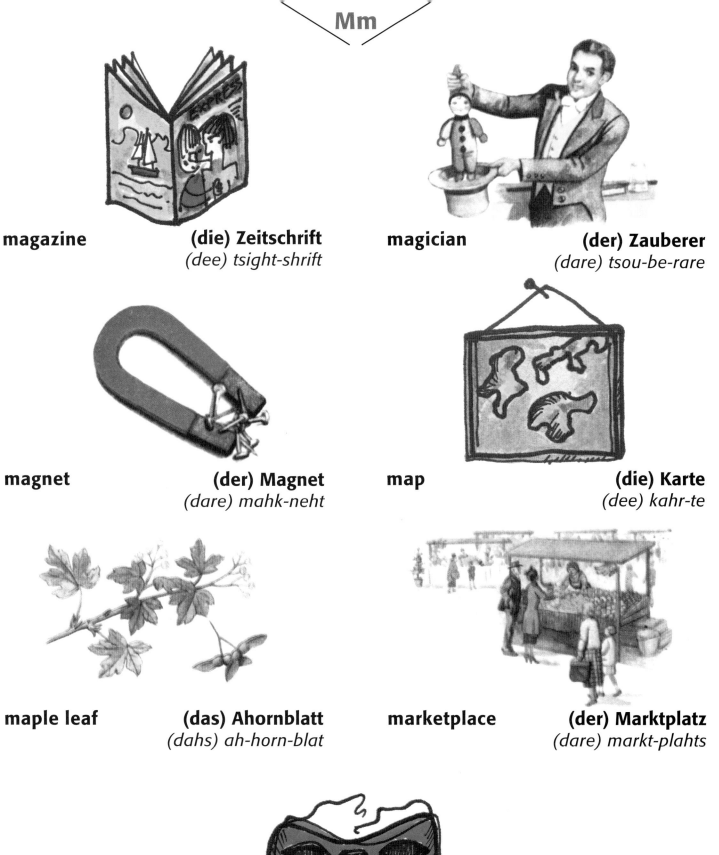

magazine   **(die) Zeitschrift**
(dee) tsight-shrift

magician   **(der) Zauberer**
(dare) tsou-be-rare

magnet   **(der) Magnet**
(dare) mahk-neht

map   **(die) Karte**
(dee) kahr-te

maple leaf   **(das) Ahornblatt**
(dahs) ah-horn-blat

marketplace   **(der) Marktplatz**
(dare) markt-plahts

mask   **(die) Maske**
(dee) mahs-ke

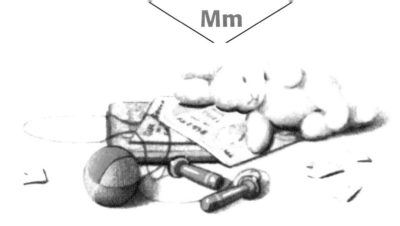

messy

unordentlich
oon-or-dent-likh

milkman
(der) Milchmann
(dare) milkh-mahn

mirror
(der) Spiegel
(dare) shpee-gel

mitten
(der) Fausthandschuh
(dare) foust-hahnt-shoo

money
(das) Geld
(dahs) gelt

monkey
(der) Affe
(dare) af-fe

moon
(der) Mond
(dare) mohnt

mother   **(die) Mutter**
(dee) moot-tare

mountain   **(der) Berg**
(dare) berk

mouse   **(die) Maus**
(dee) mous

mouth   **(der) Mund**
(dare) moont

mushroom   **(der) Pilz**
(dare) pilts

music   **(die) Musik**
(dee) moo-seek

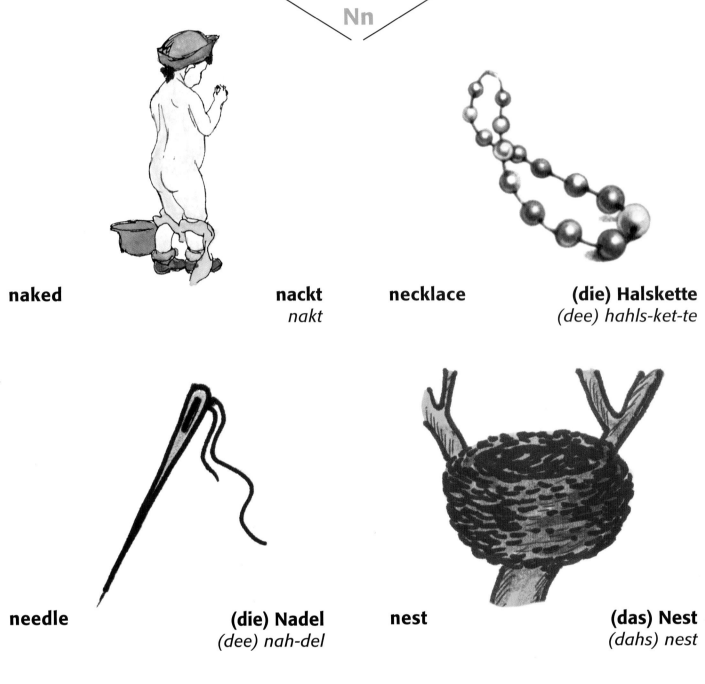

naked | **nackt**
nakt

necklace | **(die) Halskette**
(dee) hahls-ket-te

needle | **(die) Nadel**
(dee) nah-del

nest | **(das) Nest**
(dahs) nest

newspaper | **(die) Zeitung**
(dee) tsigh-toonk

nightingale **(die) Nachtigall**
(dee) nach-tee-gahl

nine **neun**
noyn

notebook **(das) Notizbuch**
(dahs) noh-teets-booch

number **(die) Zahl**
(dee) tsahl

nut **(die) Nuss**
(dee) noos

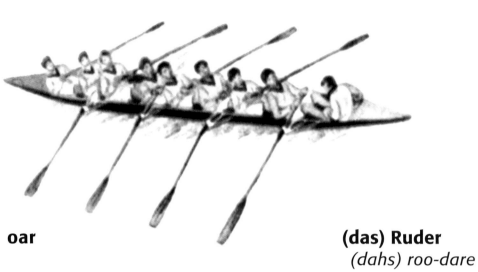

oar   **(das) Ruder**
(dahs) roo-dare

ocean liner   **(der) Ozeandampfer**
(dare) oh-tse-ahn-dahm-pfare

old   **alt**
ahlt

one   **eins**
eins

onion   **(die) Zwiebel**
(dee) tsvee-bel

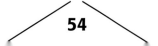

open

offen
of-fen

orange

(die) Orange
(dee) oh-rahn-je

ostrich

(der) Strauß
(dare) shtrous

owl

(die) Eule
(dee) oy-le

ox

(der) Ochse
(dare) o-xe

padlock **(das) Vorhängeschloss**
(dahs) fohr-hayn-ge-shlos

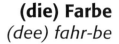

paint **(die) Farbe**
(dee) fahr-be

painter **(der) Maler**
(dare) mah-lare

pajamas **(der) Schlafanzug**
(dare) shlahf-ahn-tsook

palm tree **(die) Palme**
(dee) pahl-me

paper **(das) Papier**
(dahs) pa-peer

parachute **(der) Fallschirm**
(dare) fal-shirm

park **(der) Park**
(dare) pahrk

parrot **(der) Papagei**
(dare) pah-pah-gigh

passport **(der) Reisepass**
(dare) righ-ze-pas

patch **(der) Flicken**
(dare) flik-ken

path **(der) Weg**
(dare) vehk

peach **(der) Pfirsich**
(dare) pfir-zikh

pear **(die) Birne**
(dee) bir-ne

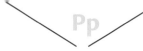

pebble

(der) Kieselstein
(dare) kee-sel-shtine

(to) peck　　　　**picken**
pik-ken

(to) peel　　　　**schälen**
shay-len

pelican　　**(der) Pelikan**
(dare) peh-li-kahn

pencil　　**(der) Bleistift**
(dare) bligh-shtift

penguin　　**(der) Pinguin**
(dare) pin-goo-een

people　　**(die) Leute**
(dee) loy-te

Pp

piano **(das) Klavier**
(dahs) klah-veer

pickle **die) Essiggurke**
(dee) es-sik-goor-ke

pie **(der) Kuchen**
(dare) koo-chen

pig **(das) Schwein**
(dahs) shvine

pigeon **(die) Taube**
(dee) tou-be

pillow **(das) Kissen**
(dahs) kis-sen

pin **(die) Stecknadel**
(dee) shtek-nah-del

pine　　　　**(die) Kiefer**
(dee) kee-fare

pineapple　　　　**(die) Ananas**
(dee) ah-nah-nahs

pit　　　　**(der) Kern**
(dare) kern

pitcher　　　　**(der) Krug**
(dare) krook

plate　　　　**(der) Teller**
(dare) tel-lare

platypus　　　　**(das) Schnabeltier**
(dahs) shnah-bel-teer

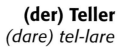

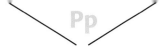

(to) play   **spielen**
shpee-len

plum   **(die) Pflaume**
(dee) pflou-me

polar bear   **(der) Eisbär**
(dare) eyes-bayr

pony   **(das) Pony**
(dahs) po-nee

pot   **(der) Topf**
(dare) topf

potato   **(die) Kartoffel**
(dee) kahr-tof-fel

(to) pour   **eingießen**
ine-gees-sen

present   **(das) Geschenk**
(dahs) ge-shenk

(to) pull   **ziehen**
tsee-hen

pumpkin   **(der) Kürbis**
(dare) koohr-bis

puppy   **(der) Welpe**
(dare) vel-pe

queen   **(die) Königin**
(dee) koe-ni-gin

rabbit

(das) Kaninchen
(dahs) kah-neen-khen

raccoon

(der) Waschbär
(dare) vash-bayr

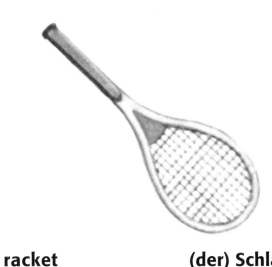

racket

(der) Schläger
(dare) shlay-gare

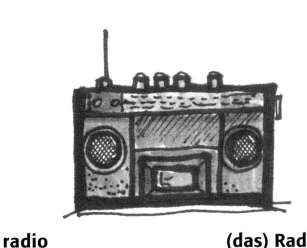

radio

(das) Radio
(dahs) rah-dee-yoh

radish

(das) Radieschen
(dahs) rah-dees-khen

raft **(das) Schlauchboot**
(dahs) shlouch-boht

rain **(der) Regen**
(dare) reh-gen

rainbow **(der) Regenbogen**
(dare) reh-gen-boh-gen

raincoat **(der) Regenmantel**
(dare) reh-gen-mahn-tel

raspberry **(die) Himbeere**
(dee) him-beh-re

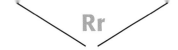

(to) read

lesen
leh-zen

red

rot
roht

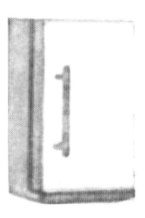

refrigerator

(der) Kühlschrank
(dare) koohl-shrank

rhinoceros

(das) Nashorn
(dahs) nahs-horn

ring

(der) Ring
(dare) ring

(to) ring   **läuten**
loy-ten

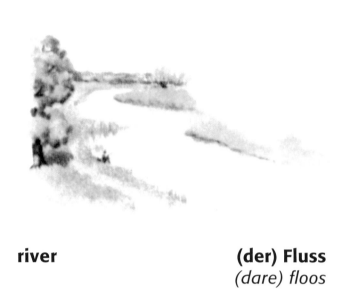

river   **(der) Fluss**
(dare) floos

road   **(die) Straße**
(dee) shtras-se

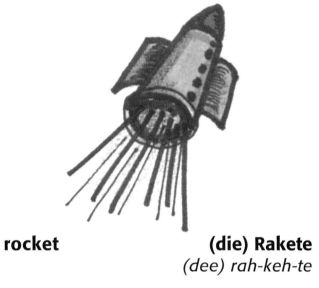

rocket   **(die) Rakete**
(dee) rah-keh-te

roof   **(das) Dach**
(dahs) dach

rooster   **(der) Hahn**
(dare) hahn

root   **(die) Wurzel**
(dee) voort-sel

rope   **(das) Seil**
(dahs) zile

rose   **(die) Rose**
(dee) roh-ze

(to) row   **rudern**
roo-dern

ruler   **(das) Lineal**
(das) lee-neh-yahl

(to) run   **rennen**
ren-nen

safety pin   **(die) Sicherheitsnadel**
(dee) zi-khare-hights-nah-del

(to) sail   **segeln**
seh-geln

sailor   **(der) Matrose**
(dare) mah-troh-ze

salt   **(das) Salz**
(dahs) sahlts

scarf   **(der) Schal**
(dare) shahl

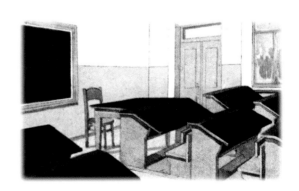

school   **(die) Schule**
(dee) shoo-le

Ss

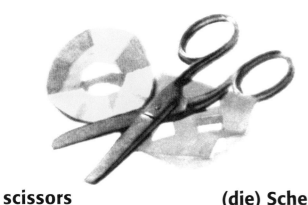

scissors **(die) Schere**
(dee) sheh-re

screwdriver **(der) Schraubenzieher**
(dare) shrou-ben-tsee-hare

seagull **(die) Möwe**
(dee) moe-ve

seesaw **(die) Wippe**
(dee) vip-pe

seven **sieben**
zee-ben

(to) sew **nähen**
nay-hen

shark (der) Haifisch
(dare) high-fish

sheep (das) Schaf
(dahs) shahf

shell (die) Muschel
(dee) moo-shel

shepherd der (Schäfer)
(dare) shay-fare

ship (das) Schiff
(dahs) shif

shirt (das) Hemd
(dahs) hemt

shoe   **(der) Schuh**
(dare) shoo

shovel   **(die) Schaufel**
(dee) shou-fel

(to) show   **zeigen**
tsigh-gen

shower   **(die) Dusche**
(dee) doo-she

shutter   **(der) Fensterladen**
(dare) fen-stare-lah-den

sick   **krank**
krahnk

sieve   **(das) Sieb**
(dahs) zeeb

(to) sing   **singen**
zin-gen

(to) sit   **sitzen**
zit-sen

six   **sechs**
zex

sled   **(der) Schlitten**
(dare) shlit-ten

(to) sleep   **schlafen**
shlah-fen

small **klein**
kline

smile **(das) Lächeln**
(dahs) lay-kheln

snail **(die) Schnecke**
(dee) shnek-ke

snake **(die) Schlange**
(dee) shlahn-ge

snow **(der) Schnee**
(dare) shneh

sock **(die) Socke**
(dee) sok-ke

sofa **(das) Sofa**
(dahs) soh-fah

sparrow **(der) Spatz**
(dare) shpats

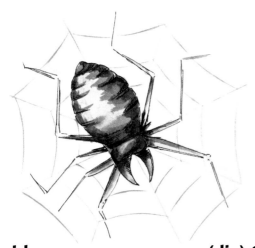

spider **(die) Spinne**
(dee) shpin-ne

spiderweb **(das) Spinnennetz**
(dahs) shpin-nen-nets

spoon **(der) Löffel**
(dare) loef-fel

squirrel **(das) Eichhörnchen**
(dahs) eikh-hoern-khen

stairs

(die) Treppe
(dee) trep-pe

stamp

(die) Briefmarke
(dee) breef-mahr-ke

starfish

(der) Seestern
(dare) seh-shtern

stork

(der) Storch
(dare) shtorkh

stove

(der) Herd
(dare) hayrt

strawberry

(die) Erdbeere
(dee) ehrd-beh-re

subway

(die) U-Bahn
(dee) oo-bahn

sugar cube **(der) Zuckerwürfel**
(dare) tsook-kare-voohr-fel

sun **(die) Sonne**
(dee) son-ne

sunflower **(die) Sonnenblume**
(dee) son-nen-bloo-me

sweater **(der) Pullover**
(dare) pool-loh-vare

(to) sweep **fegen**
feh-gen

swing **(die) Schaukel**
(dee) shou-kel

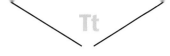
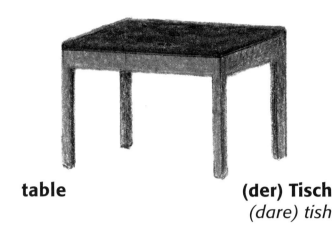

table   **(der) Tisch**
(dare) tish

teapot   **(die) Teekanne**
(dee) teh-kan-ne

teddy bear   **(der) Teddybär**
(dare) ted-dee-bayr

television   **(der) Fernseher**
(dare) fern-seh-are

ten   **zehn**
tsehn

tent   **(das) Zelt**
(dahs) tselt

theater   **(das) Theater**
(dahs) teh-ah-tare

thimble   **(der) Fingerhut**
(dare) fin-gare-hoot

(to) think   **denken**
den-ken

three   **drei**
drigh

tie   **(die) Krawatte**
(dee) krah-vat-te

(to) tie   **zuschnüren**
tsoo-shnooh-ren

tiger   **(der) Tiger**
(dare) tee-gare

toaster   **(der) Toaster**
(dare) toh-stare

tomato   **(die) Tomate**
(dee) toh-mah-te

toucan   **(der) Tukan**
(dare) too-kahn

towel   **(das) Handtuch**
(dahs) hahnt-tooch

tower   **(der) Turm**
(dare) toorm

toy box **(die) Spielzeugkiste**
(dee) shpeel-tsoyk-ki-ste

tracks **(die) Gleise**
(dee) gligh-ze

train station **(der) Bahnhof**
(dare) bahn-hohf

tray **(das) Tablett**
(dahs) tah-blet

tree **(der) Baum**
(dare) boum

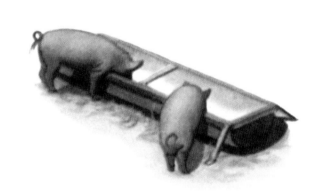

trough **(der) Trog**
(dare) trohk

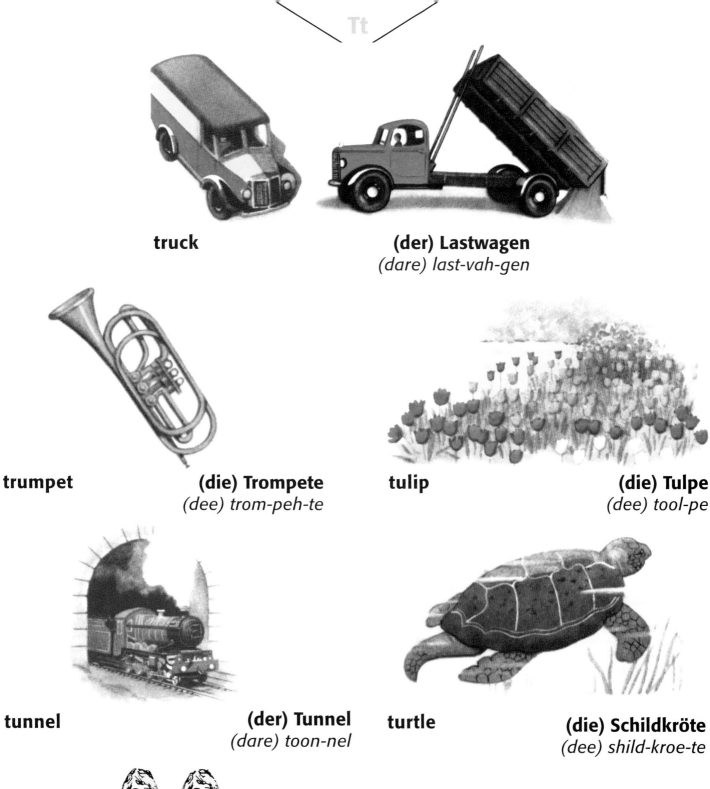

truck

(der) Lastwagen
(dare) last-vah-gen

trumpet

(die) Trompete
(dee) trom-peh-te

tulip

(die) Tulpe
(dee) tool-pe

tunnel

(der) Tunnel
(dare) toon-nel

turtle

(die) Schildkröte
(dee) shild-kroe-te

twins

(die) Zwillinge
(dee) tsvil-lin-ge

two

zwei
tsvigh

umbrella **(der) Regenschirm**
(dare) reh-gen-shirm

uphill **bergauf**
berk-ouf

vase **(die) Vase**
(dee) vah-ze

veil **(der) Schleier**
(dare) shligh-are

village

(das) Dorf
(dahs) dorf

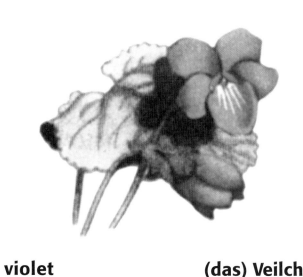

violet

(das) Veilchen
(dahs) file-khen

violin

(die) Geige
(dee) gigh-ge

voyage

(die) Fahrt
(dee) fahrt

waiter　　　　　**(der) Kellner**
(dare) kel-nare

(to) wake up　　　　**aufwachen**
ouf-vah-chen

walrus　　　　　**(das) Walross**
(dahs) vahl-ros

(to) wash　　　　**waschen**
vah-shen

watch　　　　　**(die) Uhr**
(dee) oor

(to) watch　　　　**beobachten**
beh-ohb-ach-ten

(to) water   **gießen**
gees-sen

waterfall   **(der) Wasserfall**
(dare) vas-sare-fal

watering can   **(die) Gießkanne**
(dee) gees-kan-ne

watermelon   **(die) Wassermelone**
(dee) vas-sare-meh-loh-ne

weather vane   **(der) Wetterhahn**
(dare) vet-tare-hahn

(to) weigh   **wiegen**
vee-gen

whale **(der) Wal**
(dare) vahl

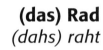

wheel **(das) Rad**
(dahs) raht

wheelbarrow **(der) Schubkarren**
(dare) shoob-kar-ren

whiskers **(die) Schnurrhaare**
(dee) shnoor-hah-re

(to) whisper **flüstern**
flooh-stern

whistle **(die) Trillerpfeife**
(dee) tril-lare-pfigh-fe

white **weiß**
vice

wig **(die) Perücke**
(dee) pare-roohk-ke

wind **(der) Wind**
(dare) vint

window **(das) Fenster**
(dahs) fen-stare

wings **(die) Flügel**
(dee) flooh-gel

winter **(der) Winter**
(dare) vin-tare

wolf **(der) Wolf**
(dare) volf

wood **(das) Holz**
(dahs) holts

word **(das) Wort**
(dahs) vort

(to) write **schreiben**
shrigh-ben

yellow

gelb
gelp

Zz

zebra

(das) Zebra
(dahs) tseh-brah

Index

A

acht	eight
Adler (der)	eagle
Affe (der)	monkey
Ahornblatt (das)	maple leaf
Alligator (der)	alligator
Alphabet (das)	alphabet
alt	old
Ananas (die)	pineapple
angeln	(to) fish
Angst (die)	fear
Antilope (die)	antelope
Apfel (der)	apple
Aquarium (das)	aquarium
Armband (das)	bracelet
Ast (der)	branch
Aubergine (die)	eggplant
Auf Wiedersehen	"Good-bye"
auflecken	(to) lap
aufwachen	(to) wake up
Auge (das)	eye
Auto (das)	car
Autobahn (die)	highway

B

Baby (das)	baby
Bäcker (der)	baker
Bahnhof (der)	train station
Ball (der)	ball
Banane (die)	banana
Bank (die)	bench
Bär (der)	bear
Bauklötze (die)	blocks
Baum (der)	tree
Bein (das)	leg
beobachten	(to) watch
Berg (der)	mountain
bergauf	uphill
Besen (der)	broom
Bett (das)	bed
Bettdecke (die)	comforter
Biber (der)	beaver
Biene (die)	bee

Birne (die)	pear
Blatt (das)	leaf
blau	blue
Bleistift (der)	pencil
Blume (die)	flower
Blüte (die)	blossom
Bonbon (das)	candy
Boot (das)	boat
braun	brown
Briefmarke (die)	stamp
Briefumschlag (der)	envelope
Brille (die)	glasses
Brot (das)	bread
Brücke (die)	brother
Brunnen (der)	fountain
Buch (das)	book
Bügeleisen (das)	iron
Bürste (die)	brush

C

Café (das)	café
Clown (der)	clown

D

Dach (das)	roof
Dachs (der)	badger
Datum (das)	date
Delphin (der)	dolphin
denken	(to) think
Dorf (das)	village
Drache (der)	dragon
drei	three
Dusche (die)	shower

E

Ei (das)	egg
Eichhörnchen (das)	squirrel
Eieruhr (die)	hourglass
Eimer (der)	bucket
eingießen	(to) pour
eins	one
Eisbär (der)	polar bear
Eis (das)	ice cream
Eislaufen	ice-skating

Eiswürfel (die)	ice cubes
Elefant (der)	elephant
Ellbogen (der)	elbow
Ente (die)	duck
Erdbeere (die)	strawberry
erforschen	(to) explore
Ernte (die)	harvest
Esel (der)	donkey
Eskimo (der)	Eskimo
essen	(to) eat
Essiggurke (die)	pickle
Eule (die)	owl

F

Fahrrad (das)	bicycle
Fahrt (die)	voyage
Fallschirm (der)	parachute
Farbe (die)	paint
Farn (der)	fern
Fass (das)	barrel
Faust (die)	fist
Fausthandschuh (der)	mitten
Feder (die)	feather
fegen	(to) sweep
Feld (das)	field
Feldmaus (die)	field mouse
Fenster (das)	window
Fensterladen (der)	shutter
Fernglas (das)	binoculars
Fernseher (der)	television
Feuer (das)	fire
Finger (der)	finger
Fingerhut (der)	thimble
Fisch (der)	fish
Flagge (die)	flag
Flasche (die)	bottle
Fledermaus (die)	bat
Flicken (der)	patch
Flieder (der)	lilac
fliegen	(to) fly
Flügel (die)	wings
Flugzeug (das)	airplane

Fluss (der) river
flüstern (to) whisper
Freund (der) friend
Frosch (der) frog
Frühstück (das) breakfast
Fuchs (der) fox
fünf five
Fuß (der) foot
füttern (to) feed

G

Gabel (die) fork
Gans (die) goose
Gardine (die) curtain
Garten (der) garden
geben (to) give
Geige (die) violin
gelb yellow
Geld (das) money
Gepäck (das) luggage
Geranie (die) geranium
Gerste (die) barley
Geschenk (das) present
Gesicht (das) face
Gewächshaus (das) greenhouse
Geweih (das) antlers
gießen (to) water
Gießkanne (die) watering can
Giraffe (die) giraffe
Gitarre (die) guitar
Glas (das) glass
Gleise (die) tracks
Globus (der) globe
Glocke (die) bell
Glühbirne (die) lightbulb
Goldfisch (der) goldfish
Grashüpfer (der) grasshopper
Großmutter (die) grandmother
Großvater (der) grandfather
grün green
Gurke (die) cucumber

Gürtel (der) belt
Gute Nacht "Good night"

H

Hahn (der) rooster
Haifisch (der) shark
Halskette (die) necklace
Hammer (der) hammer
Hamster (der) hamster
Hand (die) hand
Handschuh (der) glove
Handtasche (die) handbag
Handtuch (das) towel
Hängematte (die) hammock
Haus (das) house
Hemd (das) shirt
Henne (die) hen
Herbst (der) autumn
Herd (der) stove
Herz (das) heart
Heu (das) hay
Himbeere (die) raspberry
Höhle (die) cave
Holz (das) wood
Holzfäller (der) lumberjack
Honig (der) honey
Hörner (die) horns
Hufeisen (das) horseshoe
Hummel (die) bumblebee
Hummer (der) lobster
Hund (der) dog
Hundehütte (die) doghouse
Hut (der) hat
Hydrant (der) hydrant

I

Igel (der) hedgehog
Insel (die) island
Instrument (das) instrument
Iris (die) iris

J

Jacke (die) jacket
Jockey (der) jockey
Jongleur (der) juggler
Junge (der) boy

K

Käfer (der) beetle
Kaktus (der) cactus
Kamel (das) camel
Kamera (die) camera
Kamm (der) comb
Kängeruh (das) kangaroo
Kaninchen (das) rabbit
Kanu (das) canoe
Kapitän (der) captain
Karotte (die) carrot
Karte (die) map
Kartoffel (die) potato
Käse (der) cheese
Kätzchen (das) kitten
Katze (die) cat
Kellner (der) waiter
Kern (der) pit
Kerze (die) candle
Kiefer (die) pine
Kieselstein (der) pebble
Kirsche (die) cherry
Kissen (das) pillow
Klavier (das) piano
Kleid (das) dress
klein small
klettern (to) climb
Knochen (der) bone
Knoten (der) knot
Koalabär (der) koala bear
kochen (to) cook
Kohl (der) cabbage
Kokosnuss (die) coconut
Kompass (der) compass
Königin (die) queen
Kopfschmuck (der) headdress

Korb (der) basket
Korken (der) cork
krabbeln (to) crawl
Kräcker (der) cracker
krank sick
Krawatte (die) tie
Krone (die) crown
Krug (der) pitcher
Kuchen (der) pie
Kuh (die) cow
Kühlschrank (der) refrigerator
Kürbis (der) pumpkin
Kutsche (die) coach

L

Lächeln (das) smile
Lachen (das) laughter
Lamm (das) lamb
Lampe (die) lamp
Lastwagen (der) truck
läuten (to) ring
Lavendel (der) lavender
leer empty
Leiter (die) ladder
lesen (to) read
Leuchtturm (der) lighthouse
Leute (die) people
Libelle (die) dragonfly
Lineal (das) ruler
Löffel (der) spoon
Lokomotive (die) engine
Löwe (der) lion
Löwenzahn (der) dandelion
Luchs (der) lynx
Luftballon (der) balloon

M

Mädchen (das) girl
Magnet (der) magnet
Mais (der) corn
Maler (der) painter
Mantel (der) coat
Marienkäfer (der) ladybug
Marktplatz (der) marketplace
Marmelade (die) jam
Maske (die) mask

Matrose (der) sailor
Maus (die) mouse
Messer (das) knife
Milchmann (der) milkman
Mittagessen (das) lunch
Möbel (die) furniture
Mond (der) moon
Möwe (die) seagull
Mund (der) mouth
Muschel (die) shell
Musik (die) music
Mutter (die) mother
Mütze (die) cap

N

Nachtigall (die) nightingale
nackt naked
Nadel (die) needle
nähen (to) sew
Nashorn (das) rhinoceros
Nest (das) nest
neun nine
Notizbuch (das) notebook
Nuss (die) nut

O

Obst (das) fruit
Ochse (der) ox
offen open
Orange (die) orange
Ozeandampfer (der) ocean liner

P

Palme (die) palm tree
Papagei (der) parrot
Papier (das) paper
Park (der) park
Pelikan (der) pelican
Perücke (die) wig
Pfeil (der) arrow
Pferd (das) horse
Pfirsich (der) peach
Pflaume (die) plum

picken (to) peck
Pilz (der) mushroom
Pinguin (der) penguin
Pony (das) pony
Pullover (der) sweater
Puppe (die) doll
Puppenhaus (das) dollhouse
Puzzlespiel (das) jigsaw puzzle

R

Rad (das) wheel
Radieschen (das) radish
Radio (das) radio
Rahmen (der) frame
Rakete (die) rocket
Rasenmäher (der) lawn mower
Regen (der) rain
Regenbogen (der) rainbow
Regenmantel (der) raincoat
Regenschirm (der) umbrella
Reh (das) deer
Reisepass (der) passport
rennen (to) run
Ring (der) ring
Ritter (der) knight
Rolltreppe (die) escalator
Rose (die) rose
rot red
Rucksack (der) backpack
Ruder (das) oar
rudern (to) row

S

Salat (der)	lettuce
Salz (das)	salt
sammeln	(to) gather
Schaf (das)	sheep
Schäfer (der)	shepherd
Schal (der)	scarf
schälen	(to) peel
Schaufel (die)	shovel
Schaukel (die)	swing
Schere (die)	scissors
Schiff (das)	ship
Schildkröte (die)	turtle
Schlafanzug (der)	pajamas
schlafen	(to) sleep
Schläger (der)	racket
Schlange (die)	snake
Schlauchboot (das)	raft
Schleier (der)	veil
Schlitten (der)	sled
Schloss (das)	castle
Schlüssel (der)	key
Schmetterling (der)	butterfly
schmutzig	dirty
Schnabeltier (das)	platypus
Schnecke (die)	snail
Schnee (der)	snow
Schnurrhaare (die)	whiskers
Schokolade (die)	chocolate
Schornstein (der)	chimney
Schraubenzieher (der)	screwdriver
schreiben	(to) write
Schreibtisch (der)	desk
Schubkarren (der)	wheelbarrow
Schuh (der)	shoe
Schule (die)	school
Schüssel (die)	bowl
schwarz	black
schwarze Brett (das)	bulletin board
Schwein (das)	pig
sechs	six
Seestern (der)	starfish
segeln	(to) sail
Seil (das)	rope

sich verstecken	(to) hide
Sicherheitsnadel (die)	safety pin
Sieb (das)	sieve
sieben	seven
singen	(to) sing
sitzen	(to) sit
Socke (die)	sock
Sofa (das)	sofa
Sonne (die)	sun
Sonnenblume (die)	sunflower
Spatz (der)	sparrow
Spiegel (der)	mirror
spielen	(to) play
Spielkarte (die)	card
Spielzeugkiste (die)	toy box
Spinne (die)	spider
Spinnennetz (das)	spiderweb
springen	(to) jump
Stecknadel (die)	pin
Stiefel (der)	boot
Storch (der)	stork
Strand (der)	beach
Straße (die)	road
Strauß (der)	ostrich
stricken	(to) knit
Stuhl (der)	chair

T

Tablett (das)	tray
Tanne (die)	fir tree
tanzen	(to) dance
Taschenlampe (die)	flashlight
Taschentuch (das)	handkerchief
Taube (die)	pigeon
Taxi (das)	cab
Teddybär (der)	teddy bear
Teekanne (die)	teapot
Teller (der)	plate
Teppich (der)	carpet
Theater (das)	theater
Tiger (der)	tiger
Tisch (der)	table
Toaster (der)	toaster
Tomate (die)	tomato
Topf (der)	pot
Tor (das)	gate
Torbogen (der)	arch
Torte (die)	cake
tragen	(to) carry
treiben	(to) float
Treppe (die)	stairs
Trillerpfeife (die)	whistle
trinken	(to) drink
Trog (der)	trough
Trommel (die)	drum
Trompete (die)	trumpet
Tukan (der)	toucan
Tulpe (die)	tulip
Tunnel (der)	tunnel
Turm (der)	tower
Türschloss (das)	lock

U

U-Bahn (die)	subway
überqueren	(to) cross
Uhr (die)	watch
umarmen	(to) hug
unordentlich	messy

V

Vase (die)	vase
Vater (der)	father
Veilchen (das)	violet
Ventilator (der)	fan
vier	four
Vogel (der)	bird
Vogelkäfig (der)	birdcage
Vorhängeschloss (das)	padlock

W

Wal (der)	whale
Walross (das)	walrus
Waschbär (der)	raccoon
waschen	(to) wash
Wasserfall (der)	waterfall
Wassermelone (die)	watermelon
Weg (der)	path
Weihnachtsbaum (der)	Christmas tree
weinen	(to) cry
Weintrauben (die)	grapes
weiß	white
Wellensittich (der)	lovebird
Welpe (der)	puppy
Wetterhahn (der)	weather vane

Wiege (die)	cradle
wiegen	(to) weigh
Wind (der)	wind
Winter (der)	winter
Wippe (die)	seesaw
Wolf (der)	wolf
Wolke (die)	cloud
Wort (das)	word
Wurzel (die)	root
Wüste (die)	desert

Z

Zahl (die)	number
Zauberer (der)	magician
Zaun (der)	fence
Zebra (das)	zebra
zehn	ten
zeichnen	(to) draw
zeigen	(to) show
Zeitschrift (die)	magazine
Zeitung (die)	newspaper
Zelt (das)	tent
Ziege (die)	goat
ziehen	(to) pull
Zirkus (der)	circus
Zitrone (die)	lemon
Zuckerwürfel (der)	sugar cube
zuhören	(to) listen
zuschnüren	(to) tie
zwei	two
Zwiebel (die)	onion
Zwillinge (die)	twins

Folk Tales from Bohemia
Adolf Wenig

This folk tale collection is one of a kind, focusing uniquely on humankind's struggle with evil in the world. Delicately ornate red and black text and illustrations set the mood.

Ages 9 and up

90 pages • red and black illustrations • 5 1/2 x 8 1/4 • 0-7818-0718-2 • W • $14.95hc • (786)

Czech, Moravian and Slovak Fairy Tales
Parker Fillmore

Fifteen different classic, regional folk tales and 23 charming illustrations whisk the reader to places of romance, deception, royalty, and magic.

Ages 12 and up

243 pages • 23 b/w illustrations • 5 1/2 x 8 1/4 • 0-7818-0714-X • W • $14.95 hc • (792)

Glass Mountain: Twenty-Eight Ancient Polish Folk Tales and Fables
W.S. Kuniczak

Illustrated by Pat Bargielski

As a child in a far-away misty corner of Volhynia, W.S. Kuniczak was carried away to an extraordinary world of magic and illusion by the folk tales of his Polish nurse.

171 pages • 6 x 9 • 8 illustrations • 0-7818-0552-X • W • $16.95hc • (645)

Old Polish Legends
Retold by F.C. Anstruther

Wood engravings by J. Sekalski

This fine collection of eleven fairy tales, with an introduction by Zymunt Nowakowski, was first published in Scotland during World War II.

66 pages • 7 1/4 x 9 • 11 woodcut engravings • 0-7818-0521-X • W • $11.95hc • (653)

Folk Tales from Russia
by Donald A. Mackenzie

With nearly 200 pages and 8 full-page black-and-white illustrations, the reader will be charmed by these legendary folk tales that symbolically weave magical fantasy with the historic events of Russia's past.

Ages 12 and up

192 pages • 8 b/w illustrations • 5 1/2 x 8 1/4 • 0-7818-0696-8 • W • $12.50hc • (788)

Fairy Gold: A Book of Classic English Fairy Tales
Chosen by Ernest Rhys

Illustrated by Herbert Cole

Forty-nine imaginative black and white illustrations accompany thirty classic tales, including such beloved stories as "Jack and the Bean Stalk" and "The Three Bears."

Ages 12 and up

236 pages • 5 1/2 x 8 1/4 • 49 b/w illustrations • 0-7818-0700-X • W • $14.95hc • (790)

Tales of Languedoc: From the South of France
Samuel Jacques Brun
For readers of all ages, here is a masterful collection of folk tales from the south of France.
Ages 12 and up
248 pages • 33 b/w sketches • 5 1/2 x 8 1/4 • 0-7818-0715-8 • W • $14.95hc • (793)

Twenty Scottish Tales and Legends
Edited by Cyril Swinson
Illustrated by Allan Stewart
Twenty enchanting stories take the reader to an extraordinary world of magic harps, angry giants, mysterious spells and gallant Knights.
Ages 9 and up
215 pages • 5 1/2 x 8 1/4 • 8 b/w illustrations • 0-7818-0701-8 • W • $14.95 hc • (789)

Swedish Fairy Tales
Translated by H. L. Braekstad
A unique blending of enchantment, adventure, comedy, and romance make this collection of Swedish fairy tales a must-have for any library.
Ages 9 and up
190 pages • 21 b/w illustrations • 51/2 x 81/4 • 0-7818-0717-4 • W • $12.50hc • (787)

The Little Mermaid and Other Tales
Hans Christian Andersen
Here is a near replica of the first American edition of 27 classic fairy tales from the masterful Hans Christian Andersen.
Ages 9 and up
508 pages • b/w illustrations • 6 x 9 • 0-7818-0720-4 • W • $19.95hc • (791)

Pakistani Folk Tales: Toontoony Pie and Other Stories
Ashraf Siddiqui and Marilyn Lerch
Illustrated by Jan Fairservis
In these 22 folk tales are found not only the familiar figures of folklore—kings and beautiful princesses—but the magic of the Far East, cunning jackals, and wise holy men.
Ages 7 and up
158 pages • 6 1/2 x 8 1/2 • 38 illustrations • 0-7818-0703-4 • W • $12.50hc • (784)

Folk Tales from Chile
Brenda Hughes
This selection of 15 tales gives a taste of the variety of Chile's rich folklore. Fifteen charming illustrations accompany the text.
Ages 7 and up
121 pages • 5 1/2 x 8 1/4 • 15 illustrations • 0-7818-0712-3 • W • $12.50hc • (785)

All prices subject to change. **To purchase Hippocrene Books** contact your local bookstore, call (718) 454-2366, or write to: HIPPOCRENE BOOKS, 171 Madison Avenue, New York, NY 10016. Please enclose check or money order, adding $5.00 shipping (UPS) for the first book and $.50 for each additional book.

DISCARDED

ADAMSVILLE-COLLIER
HEIGHTS

J 433.21 HIPPOCRENE A-COLL
Hippocrene children's
illustrated German
dictionary

Atlanta-Fulton Public Library

DEC 0 1 1999